TO:

FROM:

Copyright © 2010 Hallmark Licensing, LLC

Published by Hallmark Books,
a division of Hallmark Cards, Inc.,
Kansas City, MO 64141
Visit us on the Web at Hallmark.com.

Editor: Emily Osborn
Art Director: Kevin Swanson
Designer: Mark Voss
Production Designer: Bryan Ring

ISBN: 978-1-59530-294-6

BOK2108

Printed and bound in China

NOW YOU'RE 50!

BY BRANDON CROSE

Hallmark
gift books

When John F. Kennedy accepted his party's nomination for President, he spoke of "a New Frontier...of unknown opportunities and perils, the frontier of unfilled hopes and unfilled threats." You were born during the tail end of the Baby Boom, and unlike older Boomers, you have few memories of innocent suburban bliss. The war in Vietnam was already unpopular by the time you knew what it was, "flower power" had given way to drugs and race riots, and your first civics lesson was President Richard Nixon resigning from office. Yet you did share one thing with your generation: a willingness to embrace change. Though the sky seemed dark, you truly were on the edge of a New Frontier...

WHEN YOU WERE
BORN

IN THE NEWS

Senator John F. Kennedy, a World War II hero from a large Irish–Catholic family, became the 35th President of the United States.

After tens of thousands of East German refugees fled to West Berlin to escape communist rule, the German Democratic Republic erected a wire fence to divide East Berlin from West. This simple fence would later become an 11-foot concrete barrier known as the Berlin Wall.

In Alabama, racial violence raged: Freedom Riders were savagely beaten by white mobs in Birmingham, and martial law was declared in Montgomery after a crowd of both adults and children began throwing stones through the windows of a church where Dr. Martin Luther King, Jr., was speaking.

Fear of nuclear annihilation almost became fact for thirteen very tense days as superpower leaders President John F. Kennedy and Soviet Premier Nikita Khrushchev negotiated the Cuban Missile Crisis.

Alan B. Shepard was the first American in space—*his flight lasted 15 minutes.*

EVENTS

If you were born in the south or southwest, you may have central air to thank—the spreading popularity of air conditioning made living through those humid summers a more bearable prospect for many families.

It was a time of modern wonder for your parents: the electric toothbrush hit the market, the measles vaccine was perfected… and Pampers began selling the first disposable diapers.

The Eco-Movement was born when you were: Rachel Carson's book *Silent Spring* warned (among other things) that the widespread use of DDT and other insecticides was exposing us to over 500 different chemicals.

Your mother did not take thalidomide while she was pregnant with you, thanks to Dr. Frances O. Kelsey. The morning sickness drug caused more than 10,000 deformed births in Europe, but Dr. Kelsey had denied it FDA approval in the United States.

MUSIC

You may not remember now, but "Big Bad John" by Jimmy Dean, "I Fall to Pieces" by Patsy Cline, and "Puff, the Magic Dragon" by Peter, Paul and Mary were probably among the first songs you ever heard.

Back from the Army, Elvis abandoned the youthful rock your parents danced to and composed more somber hits like "Don't Be Cruel" and "It's Now or Never."

Your parents probably never heard of The Pendletones, but they listened up when the band changed its name to The Beach Boys—"Surfin' Safari" and "Surfin' USA" were Top 20 hits.

Your parents may have also enjoyed comedian Allan Sherman's surprise hit song, "Hello Muddah, Hello Faddah." It reached number two on the billboards and stayed there for three weeks.

MOVIES

. . . .

Breakfast at Tiffany's, based on a novella
by Truman Capote, made Audrey Hepburn
a star, and may have influenced your
mother's fashion nearly as much as
Mrs. Kennedy's suits and pillbox hats.
(The theme song, "Moon River," also won
a Grammy.)

Popular movies of the time included movies you probably watched
years later—*West Side Story, A Raisin in the Sun, Birdman of
Alcatraz,* and *To Kill a Mockingbird.*

After three marriages and many movies, larger-than-life actress
(and sex symbol) Marilyn Monroe died from an overdose of
sleeping pills in her home at the age of 36.

The silver screen (and box office) stars of the time included
Elizabeth Taylor, Rock Hudson, Doris Day, John Wayne,
Cary Grant, Sandra Dee, Jerry Lewis, and Elvis Presley.

TV

FCC Chairmain Newton N. Minow called television "a vast wasteland," but that probably didn't stop your parents from tuning in to their favorite shows: *The Red Skelton Show, Bonanza, The Andy Griffith Show, Candid Camera, The Dick Van Dyke Show, The Beverly Hillbillies,* and *The Ed Sullivan Show.*

Your mother may have cooked her first omelet after seeing it done on TV. Julia Child made French cuisine accessible and interesting in *The French Chef,* which ran for 10 years.

Your father may have started watching more football when the family purchased a color TV set. The popularity of Sunday football soared once fans could see the color of their team's uniforms, and the Super Bowl was later created to give this growing audience something to cheer for.

Jackie Robinson became the first African-American inducted into the Baseball Hall of Fame.

SPORTS

New York Yankee Roger Maris made history when he hit his 61st home run against the Boston Red Sox on the final day of the 162-game season. (Babe Ruth's record was 60 home runs in a 154-game season.)

Jack Nicklaus defeated Arnold Palmer at the U.S. Open and won his first major tournament, but not his last—"The Golden Bear" went on to win a grand total of 73 PGA events during his long career.

Philadelphia Warriors basketball player Wilt Chamberlain scored a record-setting 100 points in one game to beat the New York Knicks 169–147.

POP CULTURE

For baby boys, your parents were most likely to name you Michael, David, John, James, or Robert. For baby girls, Lisa, Mary, Susan, Karen, and Linda were the most popular choices.

Your first book may have been one of Charles M. Schulz's best-sellers: *"Happiness Is a Warm Puppy"*, *"Security Is a Thumb and a Blanket"*, *"I Need All the Friends I Can Get"*, or *"Christmas Is Together-Time"*.

Cook books flew off the shelves: *"Better Homes and Gardens Nutrition for Your Family"*, *"Casserole Cook Book"*, *"The Joy of Cooking: New Edition"*, and *"The Pillsbury Family Cookbook"* were all best-sellers.

Minimum wage was $1.25, and the typical annual household income was approximately $6,000. If your mother joined (or re-joined) the workforce after you were born, her earning power was significantly less than your father's: about $1,500 a year. (But it may have helped them afford a bigger car or Swanson TV dinners.)

Your parents may have read *"The Big Honey Hunt"* to you. It was Stan and Jan Berenstain's first Berenstain Bears book—today there are hundreds of Berenstain Bears titles.

WHEN YOU WERE
A KID

IN THE NEWS

Though you were too young to serve in Vietnam, you may have known someone who did. Nearly 9 million troops served from 1964–1973, during which time over 58,000 Americans were killed and over 300,000 wounded.

The nation mourned the loss of several political and civil rights leaders: Malcolm X, Martin Luther King, Jr., and Robert F. Kennedy were all assassinated within a tumultuous three-year span.

President Richard Nixon was elected for his promise to restore order and for his "secret plan" to end the war.

Your family probably joined one billion other viewers (roughly one-fifth of the entire world's population!) to watch Neil Armstrong's historic "one small step."

You probably also remember the gripping seven-day saga of Apollo 13—an explosion crippled the shuttle's power, oxygen, and water supply, forcing the three astronauts to find a way to return home with very limited resources.

AMERICA SALUTES FIRST MEN ON THE MOON

ARMSTRONG COLLINS ALDRIN

APOLLO XI

JULY 1969

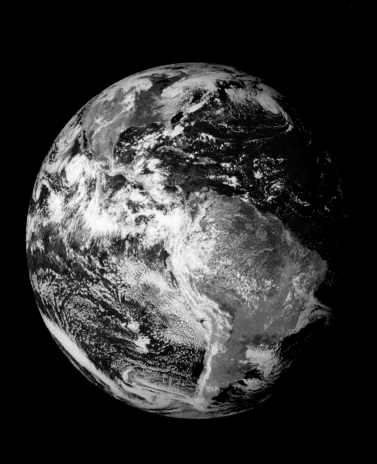

EVENTS

If your parents purchased a new car after 1966, it came equipped with seat beats (in all seats) and shatter-resistant windshields. Consumer advocate Ralph Nader's book *"Unsafe at Any Speed"* played a large part in making these safety standards law.

For better or…weird…modern science found its way into your home. From the electric styling comb (which blew warm air) to heated waterbeds to the reconstituted potato chips known as "Pringles" to the microwave oven…the future had arrived!

Residents of Coffeyville, Kansas, will not forget a September 3, 1970, storm that dropped hailstones weighing over a pound. The largest one recovered had a diameter of 5.7 inches, a circumference of 17.5 inches, and weighed 1.67 pounds!

Perhaps you and your parents were among the 20 million people to take Wednesday, April 22, off from work and school to celebrate the first Earth Day. Growing national interest in our environment soon paved the way for the Clean Air and Clean Water Acts.

MUSIC

The Monkees, a fictional TV band modeled after The Beatles' early years, had several hit songs, including "Last Train to Clarksville," "I'm a Believer," and "A Little Bit Me, A Little Bit You." Following suit, The Partridge Family hit the radio with "I Think I Love You."

Some of your other favorite songs might have included "Sugar, Sugar" by The Archies, "Ain't No Mountain High Enough" by Diana Ross, and "You've Got a Friend" by Carole King.

If you loved The Jackson 5, you were not alone. "I Want You Back," "ABC," "The Love You Save," and "I'll Be There" all hit the top of the charts less than a year after the group's debut. Stickers, posters, sew-on patches, and coloring books soon followed—there was even a Saturday morning cartoon on ABC called *Jackson 5ive*.

The Beatles gave an impromptu public performance on the roof of their Savile Row recording studio. It would turn out to be their last.

MOVIES

You may have wanted to be a singing, dancing von Trapp child after seeing *The Sound of Music* for the first time.

Walt Disney—creator (and voice) of Mickey Mouse, pioneer of the feature-length cartoon, and founder of an entertainment empire—died from lung cancer at the age of 65.

Your childhood was not without Disney, however—Roy Disney (Walt's older brother) kept the company moving forward. You may have seen *The Jungle Book*, *The Aristocats*, and *Bedknobs and Broomsticks* when they were first in theaters.

To prevent you and your friends from seeing inappropriate movies such as *Midnight Cowboy*, the Motion Picture Association of American introduced film ratings: G for General Audiences, M for Mature Audiences, R for Restricted, and X for No One Under 17.

TV

Even if you watched TV in black and white well into your late childhood, you still had some great shows: *Batman, Star Trek, Mission: Impossible, Get Smart, The Brady Bunch, H.R. Pufnstuf, Scooby Doo, Flipper,* and *Masterpiece Theatre.*

You and your parents may have watched the Nixon vs. Humphrey televised debates, or the last episode of *The Fugitive* (along with 25 million other households).

If you ever said, "Sock it to me," "Here come de judge," or "You bet your sweet bippy," then you definitely watched *Rowan & Martin's Laugh-In.* Call someone a "meathead" or "dingbat"? You dug *All in the Family.*

Over 40 million homes had a television set, and by the early '70s, half of those homes watched TV in color.

SPORTS

Whether or not you agreed that it was the "Eighth Wonder of the World," the Houston Astrodome was massive, climate controlled, and the first sports stadium to feature a roof.

The 1968 Winter Olympic Games was the first to be broadcast live and in color, but what you probably remember most is the free-skating program that won Peggy Fleming the gold medal.

Assuming that their male audience would rather watch football than *The Carol Burnett Show*, ABC launched *Monday Night Football* with announcers Howard Cosell, Keith Jackson, and Don Meredith.

Billie Jean King scored a victory for women everywhere (and female athletes in particular) when she humbled Bobby Riggs in an exhibition tennis match billed as the "Battle of the Sexes."

The Houston Astrodome was the first sports stadium to feature a roof.

POP CULTURE

It was a great time to be a kid: you could beg your parents for an American Flyer bicycle, wild-haired Troll dolls, a Rubik's Cube, or the much-coveted Batman Utility Belt, which included a plastic dart gun, Bat-cuffs, and of course, a Bat-a-rang.

Girls already had Barbie, but what about boys? Enter G.I. Joe: nearly a foot high, with 21 moving parts and a plethora of optional costumes and accessories. (Just don't call him a "doll.")

Silly String hit stores, everyone owned a Frisbee, and even break-fast was more fun—let's not forget Pop-Tarts and Lucky Charms!

Now Mickey Mouse had two homes! Disney World opened its doors in Orlando with 26 attractions—including "It's a Small World," "Country Bear Jamboree," "Swiss Family Treehouse," and "Haunted Mansion."

WHEN YOU WERE
A TEENAGER

IN THE NEWS

The Vietnam War came to a dramatic conclusion as over 1,000 American civilians and nearly 7,000 South Vietnamese refugees were evacuated from the roof of the U.S. Embassy in Saigon over the course of 18 hours. Communist forces took the city shortly after and later renamed it Ho Chi Minh City.

One day after his inauguration, President Jimmy Carter made good on a campaign promise by extending a presidential pardon to all draft dodgers.

A partial meltdown at a nuclear power plant less than ten miles from Harrisburg, Pennsylvania (and one-hundred miles from Washington, D.C.), caused nationwide panic. Three Mile Island is now cited as the worst nuclear accident in American history.

"Where were you when the mountain blew?" Hopefully nowhere near it. Mount St. Helens erupted with a force equal to 27,000 atomic bombs, killing 57 people and sending a drifting 16-mile high plume of ash as far as Idaho and Montana.

Mt. St. Helens erupted with a force equal to 27,000 atomic bombs, killing 57 people and sending a 16-mile high plume of ash as far as Idaho and Montana.

EVENTS

Technology seemed to be growing at an unchecked rate: grocery stores started using UPC codes to ring you up, doctors could now see your brain with a CAT scan, and a space station called "Skylab" was orbiting the Earth.

Back at home, your first telephone answering machine was there to take a message (on very small cassette tapes).

Disposable razors hit the market just in time for you to need them!

No advancement was so shocking as the announcement of the world's first baby conceived in vitro. The "test-tube baby" was born to Lesley and John Brown, an otherwise average British couple who suddenly found themselves in the center of a media maelstrom.

You may not have known it at the time, but you witnessed the dawn of the video game with Pong. Modeled after table tennis, this deceptively simple game made its creators very wealthy, and paved the way for Atari's many home consoles and games.

MUSIC

Rock 'n' Roll had evolved—and not quietly. Heavy metal bands Led Zeppelin, AC/DC, Aerosmith, and Van Halen blew out their amps (and your parents' eardrums); punk rockers The Sex Pistols, Patti Smith, The Velvet Underground, and The Ramones spoke directly to your teenaged rebellion; innovative rockers The Eagles and Fleetwood Mac changed the musical landscape.

You were too young for Woodstock, but you couldn't have missed the short-lived Disco Era. Though the craze began with the Hues Corporation's hit "Rock the Boat," no one better exemplified disco than the Bee Gees with their hits "Stayin' Alive" and "How Deep Is Your Love" from the *Saturday Night Fever* soundtrack (which sold 12 million copies).

If you saw Elvis's final tour, you were in for quite a spectacle: that white caped suit, his martial arts moves, those sweaty scarves and the manic fans who reached for them… Elvis died at the age of 42, and only one day later, heartbroken fans had purchased his records by the millions.

Other hit songs often heard on your radio (or perhaps your new Sony Walkman) included Paul Simon's "50 Ways to Leave Your Lover," Billy Joel's "Just the Way You Are," and Player's "Baby Come Back."

TV

Wonder Woman, Charlie's Angels, and *The Bionic Woman* showed America that women could be action heroes, too.

Saturday Night Live premiered, launching the careers of Bill Murray, Chevy Chase, Dan Aykroyd, Steve Martin, and many others.

If you watched anything other than *Roots* between January 23–30, 1977, then you were in the minority. An incredible 85% of the viewing public watched the 12-hour mini-series adaptation of Alex Haley's novel.

Everyone loved a sitcom: *Three's Company, Laverne and Shirley, Happy Days, Mork and Mindy,* and *M*A*S*H* were all hits.

SPORTS

Gymnast Nadia Comaneci of Romania became the first athlete to score a perfect 10.0 at the Olympic games. Not bad for a 14-year-old!

Former Olympic champion Leon Spinks challenged Muhammad Ali for the World Heavyweight Title and won it in a split decision. Ali, however, regained the title seven months later.

There's a reason he was the world's top-earning tennis player by the end of the decade—Björn Borg won a record five consecutive Wimbledon Singles Championships between 1976–1980.

Björn Borg won a record
five consecutive Wimbledon
Singles Championships
between 1976–1980.

POP CULTURE

Tom Wolfe called it the "Me Decade," but you were just having fun! Mood rings were in, Pet Rocks were the perfect gift, your car probably had bumper stickers all over it, and your T-shirts sported the names and logos of your favorite bands.

The Disco Era brought flashing lights, spinning mirror balls, and polyester clothes. Perhaps you still have your favorite leisure suit in a closet somewhere?

Even if you didn't join in on the anti-nuclear rallies, you probably still had a healthy distrust of unnatural chemicals. Sales of health food rose from $140 million in 1970 to $1.6 billion in 1979!

If you were looking forward to trying a can of Billy Beer, you may have had to wait a bit longer—Massachusetts and several other states raised the legal drinking age from 18 to 20. (And by the time you were 20, Billy Beer had probably gone out of business.)

If you exchanged vows right out of high school, you faced some sobering statistics—the divorce rate had increased by 69% since 1968. The average marriage lasted 6.6 years.

WHEN YOU WERE
IN YOUR 20s

IN THE NEWS

If you depended on the federal government for student financial aid, food stamps, or Aid to Families with Dependent Children (AFDC), you were likely not pleased with President Ronald Reagan's budget cuts. An estimated 20 to 25 million people living just above the poverty line either lost their federal aid or saw it severely reduced.

Millions watched in horror as the space shuttle Challenger—whose crew included Christa McAuliffe, a school teacher— exploded moments after takeoff.

You weren't old enough to remember when the wall went up, but you definitely remember when it came down: The Cold War came to a symbolic end with the fall of the Berlin Wall.

George H.W. Bush accepted his party's nomination at the Republican National Convention by making a pledge that would later haunt his presidency: "Read my lips—no new taxes."

Over one million people took to the streets of New York City to join the largest anti-nuclear demonstration in history.

EVENTS

Tired of the looming threat of nuclear disaster, and still shaken by the partial core meltdown at Three Mile Island, over one million people took to the streets of New York City to join the largest anti-nuclear demonstration in history.

The Nintendo Entertainment System picked up where your Atari 2600 left off. "Mario" and "Zelda" became household names as the gray and black box sold over 60 million units in its first two years.

You may have purchased a new Cometron or Comet Catcher telescope to watch the once-in-a-lifetime passing of Halley's Comet in 1986. This orbiting ball of ice and dust passes Earth approximately once every 76 years, despite Pope Calixtus III excommunicating it as an agent of the devil in 1456.

Most thought the AIDS epidemic was only a threat to homosexuals and drug addicts until 13-year-old Ryan White made his story known. He had acquired the virus through a blood transfusion.

MUSIC

· ·

If you had $900–$1,000 to burn, you may
have listened to Michael Jackson's "Thriller"
on the Sony CDP-101—the world's first
commercially released CD player.

First featured in a commercial for the California Raisin Industry,
four singing raisins spawned four albums, two TV specials, and a
host of merchandise. The shriveled superstars are now part of the
Smithsonian's permanent collection.

Think the title track to Bruce Springsteen's *Born in the USA*
is about American pride? Many did, and still do. However, "The
Boss" wrote the song about how shamefully Vietnam veterans were
treated after the war ended.

MOVIES

Blockbuster popcorn flicks reigned supreme: you probably saw *Raiders of the Lost Ark, Return of the Jedi, Ghostbusters, The Terminator,* and *Back to the Future* in the theater. Several times.

The most popular movie of the decade, however, was about a little alien with a penchant for Reese's Pieces. *E.T., the Extra-Terrestrial* sold close to 142 million tickets.

Tom Cruise became a heartthrob with *Risky Business,* and *Top Gun* inspired a fashion throwback: leather bomber and aviator jackets were popular again.

You may have thought about taking pottery lessons after seeing Patrick Swayze and Demi Moore in *Ghost.*

TV

You grew up with only three to five channels, but soon there were almost 60! Just a few years after it was introduced, more than half of American homes had cable TV. (Though some came to agree with Bruce Springsteen: "There's 57 channels and nothing on!")

Now you could watch your music, too! Sales of videocassette tapes soared with the launch of MTV, the first 24-hour music video network.

Why go to the mall? The Home Shopping Network gave you the ability to make all of your impulse purchases from the comfort of your home.

The final episode of *M*A*S*H* shattered TV records by drawing 105.97 million viewers. It held this record for 27 years—until 2010's Super Bowl XLIV.

Central Missouri State University became the first school to win NCAA Division II titles in both Men's and Women's Basketball.

SPORTS

The American star of the 1984 Olympic Games in Los Angeles was track-and-field athlete Carl Lewis, who took four gold medals.

Before his illegal betting got him ousted from baseball, Cincinnati Reds batter Pete Rose surpassed 4,191 hits to break a record set 57 years earlier by Ty Cobb.

If it hadn't yet, the widespread cocaine problem in the mid-'80s got your attention when it claimed two athletes: Len Bias, newly drafted by the Boston Celtics, and professional football player Don Rogers.

Martina Navratilova, a Czech-American joined the ranks of Billie Jean King when she won three Grand Slam singles championships in the same year, giving her the longest winning streak of any tennis player (winning 74 consecutive matches).

POP CULTURE

· ·

Trivial Pursuit was the hot new game,
plastic flowers danced to music, New Coke
was quickly replaced with Coca-Cola
Classic, either you were a "yuppie" or
you hated them, Jane Fonda and Richard
Simmons ushered in a fitness craze,
and you may have battled other parents
so your child could "adopt" a Cabbage
Patch Kids Doll.

The median annual family income was about $23,000 when you
joined the workforce; $30,000 if both spouses were working.
However, the savings and loan crisis likely made it difficult for
you to acquire financing for your first home.

You were most likely to name your children Michael, Christopher,
Matthew, Joshua, or David if boys; for girls: Jessica, Ashley,
Jennifer, Amanda, or Sarah.

WHEN YOU WERE
IN YOUR 30s

IN THE NEWS

Still reeling from race riots after the Rodney King trial just two years earlier, Los Angeles was rocked by an early morning earthquake measuring 6.6 on the Richter scale. It lasted only 40 seconds, but that was long enough to destroy several buildings and freeways, killing 55 people.

You may have read the Unabomber's manifesto in *The New York Times* or the *Washington Post*—it was jointly printed in both papers.

President Bill Clinton, despite the ongoing Whitewater investigation, was the first Democrat to win reelection since 1944.

All 51 days televised, the standoff between followers of David Koresh and federal agents at a Waco, Texas, compound ended with the deaths of over 80 people.

A historic peace agreement in Northern Ireland promised to end the terrorism and civil unrest that had plagued the region for more than eight decades.

Y2K

EVENTS

Whether or not Vice President Al Gore "invented" it, the Internet rapidly changed the way you communicated with friends and loved ones. The connection speeds were not quite so rapid, however. Remember dial-up?

Your science-fictional dreams (or fears) came true when scientists in Scotland successfully cloned a lamb named Dolly, igniting a worldwide debate about the implications of cloning technology.

Computers had changed quite a lot since your Apple II, but one thing remained the same: their internal clocks had never been programmed to recognize the year 2000. Fearing a technological apocalypse (or at least bizarre record-keeping), computer programmers raced to fix the Y2K bug.

MUSIC

Amidst accusations of sexual misconduct with a minor, Michael Jackson exchanged vows with 27-year-old Lisa Marie Presley.

Elton John rewrote an old song and performed it at the funeral of Princess Diana. "Candle in the Wind '97" quickly sold 34 million copies, and all proceeds were donated to charity.

Whitney Houston made her big-screen debut with Kevin Costner in *The Bodyguard*, and the album (which featured her international chart-topping cover of Dolly Parton's "I Will Always Love You") became the best-selling soundtrack of all time.

Two familiar bands reunited to release best-selling live albums: The Eagles' *"Hell Freezes Over"* and Fleetwood Mac's *"The Dance"* both debuted at number one on the charts.

Other hit songs from this time include Los Del Rio's "Macarena," Celine Dion's "My Heart Will Go On," and Ricky Martin's "Livin' La Vida Loca."

MOVIES

Jim Carrey became the funny man of the decade with hit movies *Ace Ventura: Pet Detective, Dumb and Dumber,* and *Liar Liar* (for which he was paid $20 million).

Denzel Washington starred in two landmark films—as the slain civil rights leader in *Malcolm X,* and a lawyer who fights to protect the rights of an HIV-positive man in *Philadelphia.*

Forrest Gump gave a new perspective to the news stories of your early childhood, and introduced the philosophy "Life is like a box of chocolates."

Everything old was new again. Movies based on the television shows of your youth included *The Brady Bunch Movie, Charlie's Angels,* and *Lost in Space.*

You probably also enjoyed *Thelma and Louise, The Piano,* and the heartrending *Schindler's List,* which earned a staggering 12 Academy Award nominations and six Oscars, including Best Director and Best Picture.

TV

. . . .

Millions watched minute-by-minute televised coverage of scandals—
from the O.J. Simpson police chase and trial to the Tonya Harding/
Nancy Kerrigan assault and even to charges of infidelity on the part
of the President.

Even if you were one of very few people who
didn't watch *Seinfeld*, you couldn't escape
your friends and co-workers quoting it
(not that there's anything wrong with that).
After nine seasons, more than 30 million
people tuned in to watch the series finale.

A former politician and successful news anchor, Jerry Springer
became better known as the host of the shockingly disturbing
(and wildly popular) *Jerry Springer Show.*

While on that couch, many potatoes enjoyed hit shows like
*America's Funniest Home Videos, Home Improvement,
Ally McBeal, Frasier,* and *ER.*

"Yadda, yadda, yadda."

SEINFELD

SPORTS

∙∙

Baseball fans deserted their teams in droves when a 257-day
strike led to the cancellation of 1994's October playoffs
and World Series.

After the strike ended, the high salaries of professional sports
players became a hot topic at the water cooler. For example, Kevin
Garnett of the Minnesota Timberwolves turned down a six-year,
$103.5 million contract. By contrast, the President of the United
States made $200,000 a year.

After stumbling in two previous Olympic competitions, American
speed skater Dan Jansen exemplified perseverance by taking home
the gold medal and setting a new world record in the 1994 Winter
Olympics' 1,000-meter event.

Basketball fans were stunned when three-
time MVP Earvin "Magic" Johnson an-
nounced that he was HIV-positive and
would retire from the NBA.

POP CULTURE

From the television you watched to the songs on the radio, popular culture seemed obsessed with youth and the young. Teen pop sensations The Backstreet Boys, Britney Spears, 'N Sync, and Christina Aguilera seemed to be everywhere; the most popular TV shows included teen-marketed *The Simpsons, Friends,* and *South Park.*

Dr. Deepak Chopra may have changed your mind about alternative medicine with his best-selling book *Ageless Body, Timeless Mind.* If so, you weren't alone—*Time* magazine even named Chopra one of the "Top 100 Icons and Heroes of the Century."

Casual yet durable clothes by L.L.Bean and Eddie Bauer were in, and if the company you worked for was one of many that now offered dress-down days, you could even wear them there!

Fanny packs were hip, emoticons put smiles in your email, books on tape let you read while driving, and you learned that *Men Are from Mars, Women Are from Venus.*

Beanie Babies

were all the rage and became
must-have collectables.

IN THE NEWS

President George W. Bush declared war on Iraq, ostensibly to find weapons of mass destruction before they could be used against America or its allies.

No one expected the devastation of Hurricane Katrina. The category four storm claimed the lives of nearly 2,000 New Orleans natives and the homes of many more.

The space shuttle Columbia unexpectedly disintegrated after its return from a successful 16-day mission. All seven astronauts were killed, and debris from the shuttle rained across hundreds of miles of Texas countryside.

From Mr. Universe to the Terminator to…California's 38th Governor? After surprising the world by announcing his candidacy on *The Tonight Show with Jay Leno,* voters elected Arnold Schwarzenegger over 134 other candidates.

September 11, 2001.
We will never forget.

EVENTS

Previously a bulky thing for affluent people (or show-offs), the cell phone evolved by leaps and bounds. Suddenly everyone had one—you learned how to send a text message, and the home phone (or "landline") became an unnecessary expense.

From humble beginnings to 44th President of the United States, Barack Obama showed the world that the American dream is very much alive.

Were you one of 50 million people without power during the Northeast Blackout of 2003? After a cascading power failure, eight U.S. states and parts of Canada were left without electricity for a day or longer.

When you heard the news, you probably thought it was a practical joke: Pluto is no longer considered a planet.

MUSIC

You listened to your music on LPs, then CDs…and now digitally!
You probably first heard about MP3s when file-sharing program
Napster came under fire for giving anyone with a computer and an
Internet connection free reign to trade music files.

American Idol launched the careers of talented performers
Kelly Clarkson, Carrie Underwood, and Chris Daughtry. (As well
as musical oddity William Hung.)

With the option to buy your music online by the song or album,
digital downloads eclipsed sales of the physical CD. Tower Records,
Virgin Records, and hundreds of independent record stores across
the country began closing their doors.

Alicia Keys was a piano-playing phenomenon, releasing four
albums (including her runaway sophomore hit, "*The Diary of
Alicia Keys*") and stacking up 12 Grammy Awards.

The way you listen to music has changed with the advent of portable MP3 players like the Apple iPod, which can easily hold your entire music library.

MOVIES

Whether you read and re-read the books or just remember seeing "Frodo Lives!" on buttons and t-shirts (and wondering what it meant), no one would deny that Peter Jackson's massively epic (and epically massive) *Lord of the Rings* film trilogy was the movie event of the decade.

Picking up where *"Silent Spring"* left off, Al Gore's *An Inconvenient Truth* raised public awareness (and debate) over environmental issues.

Audrey Tautou swept you away in *Amélie,* a fairy tale-like love story set in Paris. Even if you didn't like reading subtitles, you're probably glad you made an exception.

Thanks to her powerful performance in *Monster's Ball,* Halle Berry became the first African–American woman to win an Academy Award for Best Actress.

TV

Mega-popular "Reality TV" shows such as *Survivor, Dancing With the Stars,* and *The Apprentice* eclipsed scripted dramas and comedies.

Remember when television sets were built into really heavy wooden cabinets? Flat-screen TVs were so light that they could be mounted on your wall.

Music isn't the only thing that went digital—now you could watch TV shows on your computer. (Not recommended if you're still using dial-up…)

You had to spring for the premium cable package (or wait for the DVDs) to catch some of the best shows on television, such as *The Sopranos, Six Feet Under, Battlestar Galactica, The Wire,* and *The Shield.*

"You're fired!"

DONALD TRUMP

SPORTS

Long-beleaguered Boston Red Sox fans had their day when their team beat the St. Louis Cardinals to win their first World Series Championship in 86 years.

American cyclist Lance Armstrong survived cancer and took home seven Tour de France titles—and counting!

NASCAR fans were stunned when seven-time Winston Cup champion Dale Earnhardt suffered a fatal crash during the final lap of the Daytona 500.

The issue of steroid abuse in professional baseball came to public attention when former player Jose Canseco published a controversial memoir titled *Juiced: Wild Times, Rampant 'Roids, Smash Hits, and How Baseball Got Big.*

American swimmer Michael Phelps won eight events at the 2008 Beijing Olympics, setting a new record for the most gold medals won in a single Olympics.

POP CULTURE

Muggles of all ages made time to read about Harry Potter and his friends Ron and Hermione. J.K. Rowling's endearing books spawned several successful movies and a plethora of merchandise, but they were not loved by all—many schools banned the books for fear that they promoted witchcraft.

You probably used popular social applications such as Facebook to keep in touch; half of all Boomers maintained an online profile. (And if you didn't, everyone thought you should.)

If your children had children of their own, your grandson(s) might be named Jacob, Michael, Ethan, Joshua, or Daniel. Your granddaughter(s) might be named Emily, Emma, Isabella, Ava, or Madison.

Facebook:

A new way to keep in touch, even with people you haven't seen since high school.

NOW

MOST PEOPLE YOUR AGE ARE:

- Married, with at least some college education.
- Homeowners and employed.
- Living in California, Texas, New York, or Pennsylvania. (Or considering moving to Florida…)
- Enjoying a higher household income than any other age group.
- Worried about keeping pace with the cost of living.
- In better health than the generation before.
- Driving (or hoping to buy) a BMW, Lexus, Infiniti, or hybrid model.
- Looking forward to retiring in 15 years!

LOOK WHO ELSE IS IN THEIR 50S:

- Alec Baldwin, actor
- Annette Bening, actress
- Belinda Carlisle, singer
- Simon Cowell, English artist and producer
- Ellen Degeneres, actress and talk show host
- David Duchovny, actor
- Colin Firth, actor
- Ari Fleischer, former White House Press Secretary
- Neil Gaiman, British author
- Amy Grant, singer
- Jamie Lee Curtis, actress
- Ivan Lendl, tennis player
- Madonna, singer
- John McEnroe, tennis player
- Marie Osmond, actress and singer
- Sean Penn, actor
- Tony Robbins, motivational speaker
- Kristin Scott Thomas, actress
- "Weird Al" Yankovic, musician